T0203427

Remember

the

Details

Skye Arundhati

Thomas

Remember the Details is the second installment of the Critic's Essay Series published by Floating Opera Press. Comprising long-form essays, the series gives voice to critics who offer thought-provoking ways in which to subvert or replace normative modes of discussing culture and the world beyond.

Other essays in the series:
Queer Formalism: The Return, by William J. Simmons

Contents

An Introductory Note

Footage of the 2019 Indian people's protest movement has lived several lives. First, it flashed across social media as evidence of state brutality: shaky, unstable photographs and videos taken on smartphones of students and activists confronted by police and army officials in riot gear flooded our screens. It was later repurposed, entering courtrooms and charge sheets as key evidence against a group of unarmed young activists who were involved in the protests. This essay tracks some of this footage; it is an attempt at writing a history. Many of this history's protagonists—young women, activists, academics—are currently incarcerated, in pre-trial detention, or living under the fear of arrest. The protest sites have been demolished. The public space that had held the critical conversations produced by the movement—conversations that questioned words like "democracy" and "citizenship"—are now more intensely surveilled. The images that remain as proof of this time are being manipulated and reframed. As viewers, we have become forensic examiners, we stay with the small details, those that testify to the collective acts of resistance and their brutal suppression. These details provide a system of accountability, they are record and document, but also something else, something more abstract and intangible: their analysis affords us certain powers, powers that are necessary to counter the state's looming enormity, its absolute control. We are being asked to forget, but this essay is an attempt to remember.

I

In late November 2019, students in Guwahati, a valley city in India's northeastern state of Assam, took to the streets, holding flickering bamboo torches. Prime Minister Narendra Modi's central government was about to introduce two new laws in parliament that effectively legalized religious and caste-based discrimination. The first was the Citizenship (Amendment) Act 2019 (CAA), a revision to the Citizenship Act of 1955, which added new conditions to the granting of Indian citizenship. Modi's update included a religious classification—when granting asylum to religious minorities, it excluded Muslims. The second law was a National Register of Citizens (NRC), an addition to the National Population Register (NPR), which required Indians to provide documentation, if and when asked by local state authorities, as proof of ancestry. This targeted indigenous and lower-caste communities, who are often undocumented, with no rights to the land they occupy or work on. The two laws are designed to work in tandem: one in determining who gets to call themselves Indian, and the other in imprisoning those whose definition the state finds lacking. Detention centers were readied; in Assam, people had already been taken in under the NRC. The students of Guwahati and beyond were leading protests against the new laws, demanding their repeal. Members of the All Assam Student's Union hoisted black flags and banners, riding through the streets on their motorcycles, chanting slogans.

For three weeks, peaceful protests carried across northeast India. There were vigils, sit-ins, and marches. The CAA was passed by the Indian parliament on December 12, 2019. In Guwahati, the central government deployed the army, announced a curfew, and disabled mobile phone data and Internet networks. They kettled crowds and attempted to stop the spread of information. Despite this, images from the ground began to proliferate, mainly on social media. Photographs often appeared without much context, and certain poses, details, and captions became the subject of a deep and intense voyeurism. As viewers, we had to piece the events together. The Modi regime and its propaganda machine had branded the protestors as insurgent and riotous almost immediately, but the images that came in seemed to prove that the violence was provoked by the police.

Images from Guwahati, frequently taken on mobile phone cameras, showed students and young activists in confrontations with the police, as fires raged behind them. "Hoi CAA batil korok, nohole aamak arrest korok," they said, *either scrap the CAA or arrest us.*

The clashes were deeply uneven. The police wore riot gear—flak jackets, combat boots, helmets, shields—and carried machine guns. Protestors were unarmed, sometimes holding only their phones. State forces dragged protestors to the ground, batons darting over bent bodies; they fired automatic rounds of gunfire in the air. An Assamese journalist tweeted, "It is Hong Kong in Guwahati," because suddenly, and without warning, police guns were turned directly onto civilians. On the same day that the CAA was passed, a seventeen-year-old student named Sam Stafford was walking home from a protest site in Hatigaon, an area in the southern part of the city. The streetlights were turned off because it was past curfew. Eyewitnesses describe police vehicles stopping in front of a group of unarmed protestors. Stafford was shot in the face barely five hundred meters from his home. "They kneeled down, took position, and fired," one eyewitness described. Fifteen minutes north of this, nineteen-year-old Dipanjali Das, who was also making his way home from a protest, was shot by Army officials conducting a "search operation." At the gatherings that followed, crowds held memorials for the murdered teenagers, decorating photographs of them with cloth and delicately placed marigolds.

II.

The CAA and NRC's intentional targeting of Muslims was the latest in a slew of policies and paperwork that sought to alienate, and eventually obliterate, the Islamic history of the Indian subcontinent. The Mughal-era was being removed from school textbooks by state orders, and fake news circulated that attempted to revise that same history as violent and oppressive to Hindus. Denying India's vast and diverse Muslim legacy was also an act of negating the contemporary lived experience of Indian Muslims. The Modi regime was being systemic: erasing a past only to set the precedent for the erasure of futures to come.

But the passing of the CAA and NRC proved to be a tipping point, and a movement bloomed across the country. India was energized by a revolutionary spirit. Muslim, Dalit, and Adivasi students, activists, writers, musicians, and poets addressed crowds at twenty-four-hour sit-ins and occupations of public space. People shared snacks, and held hours-long debates about the intention of words like "citizenship" and "democracy." In large part, the protests were led by Muslim women who centered their activism on building community spaces. Women who were still required to attend to the invisible labor of the household before they could come to the protest sites; women whose children looked on, inspired by their actions. It was not a movement of patriarchs, or individuals, but a tender, lively intimacy. Small libraries and day-care centers were constructed, where adolescents and teen-agers read the writings of revolutionaries who had come before them. They recorded what they saw, making drawings and watercolors of the protest sites. The children produced portraits of their mothers, whom they depicted standing alongside magical animals and hybrid machines. Their artworks were pinned onto walls and fences, lined bus stops and metro stations; they became a living, imaginative record of the movement as it grew.

At dawn on January 17, 2020, a forty-foot-tall iron sculpture was installed by students under a footbridge on the Delhi-Noida highway, which passed through a protest site in northeast New Delhi, Shaheen Bagh. It was an outline of the map of India, and inscribed within it was a slogan: "Hum Bharat ke log CAA-NPR-NRC nahi maante." *We the people of India, say no to CAA-NPR-NRC.* Made by artists Pawan Shukla and Veer Chandra from West Bengal, the sculpture was a decisive gesture: towering and monumental. India's borders were illuminated by a flickering red neon light. The sculpture mimicked the grandstanding nature of the Modi regime's own architecture and public artworks, which are characterized by enormity and ostentation. A basket of onions was placed in front of it. That week, the price of onions had reached an all-time high. It was a simple juxtaposition to remind viewers of how the country—in particular, its agrarian labor force—was battling exorbitant and escalating inflation, news of which had been overshadowed by the citizenship laws and ensuing protests.

Not far from this iron map, another group of students installed a ten-foot cardboard replica of India Gate. The monument, located on the eastern edge of the "ceremonial axis" of New Delhi, was formerly known as the All India War Memorial and first unveiled in 1931 in memory of the 90,000 soldiers who died in service of the British Army during World War I and the Third Afghan War. Designed by Edward Lutyens—the colonial English architect responsible for the political corridors of New Delhi, its parliament house, and grand promenades—India Gate was intentionally left without any religious iconography. Its dusty red walls, made from sandstone quarried in Bharatpur, Rajasthan, are inscribed with the names of fallen soldiers. At Shaheen Bagh, the cardboard version was propped up on kiln bricks, a small Indian flag fluttering at its top. Inscribed in black marker pen down the sides, was a list of the protestors who had so far lost their lives. It was made from flimsy paper, and fought against strong wind. This seemed to capture the reality of the situation: these were the names that would not be commemorated, these were the names that the state was committed to forget.

The Modi regime led a coordinated effort to brand the protests as unlawful and violent. Tensions ran especially high in New Delhi. In February 2020, violence raged through the city's northeastern neighborhoods. Muslims were targeted by Hindu mobs, as groups of masked civilians burned down shops and threw cooking-gas bombs through windows, and at cars. Rather than stopping the bloodshed, footage from the scene showed the police watching on. Hundreds were injured, and at least seventy people are known to have died. In March 2020, the New Delhi Police filed a case claiming that the attacks were the result of a conspiracy led by a group of young activists, and a series of arrests were made in what is now knows as the "Delhi riots case."

After COVID-19 was declared a global pandemic, the central government announced a nationwide lockdown. One day after it was implemented, public officials were sent to demolish protest sites. They painted over slogans on walls; removed the artworks; destroyed the libraries and makeshift clinics; stripped away the rugs and bedding that had been carefully laid out to keep attendees warm through the long nights. The protests had built solidarities between the urban elite and those that had been on the frontlines of dissent for years previous; between people of different genders, ethnic identities, and religious beliefs. This upset the Modi regime's positioning of the Hindu nation-state as the only antidote to India's decades of communal violence and corruption. The Hindu nation-state proposed that India may only be unified under the aegis of a single identity; the protests showed that Indians thrive in the recognition and caring negotiation of their difference. That women and young students were leading the protests only further articulated the desire of many Indians to build a different future, to imagine a different system of community. This was a deeply ideological threat, one that undermined the foundations of the Modi government, and its arsenal began to do everything in its power to counter it. Systematically, the non-violent and discursive nature of the movement was reframed as riotous by the central government, state-controlled media, and a concerted spread of fake news. Many of the movement's leaders are still being held in pre-trial detention at maximum-security prisons across the country. They continue to file petitions; they are rarely granted bail.

III.

On September 16, 2020, a group of independent journalists, activists, and academics held a conference in the tree-shaded courtyard of the Press Club of India in New Delhi. A pre-recorded video was switched on. "If you are watching this," said the lone figure on the screen, "it means I have been arrested." Umar Khalid, a young Muslim activist and scholar of indigenous histories, had been taken into custody three days prior. After being interrogated for eleven hours by a special cell of the Delhi Police—assembled to investigate the Delhi riots case—he was booked under sections of the Indian Penal Code, the Prevention of Damage to Public Property Act, and the Arms Act. He was charged with rioting, conspiracy, murder, and arms trade. Allegedly, the evidence incriminating Khalid ran to a hundred thousand pages. "What is the risk I pose?" he asks in the video, continuing, "Is it that I claim this country to be as much mine as it is yours?" Dressed in a pale cotton shirt, seated in front of a blank, white wall, Khalid is speaking from the past with a warning for the future. As he talks, he gesticulates with one hand, his movements punctuating what he says: "They are trying to trap you in their lies."

In the months leading up to his arrest, Khalid had been one of the most visible figures of the anti-CAA/NRC protest movement. On February 17, 2020, he addressed a rally of primarily Muslim men in Amravati, a city in the state of Maharashtra. An attendee uploaded a video of his speech onto YouTube. In it, Khalid is invited onto stage, where he speaks about the assault of students at Jamia Millia Islamia, the National Islamic University in New Delhi, which had taken place three months before. Standing behind a red podium, with one arm on either side, he begins by thanking "the women, the mothers, the sisters, the grandmothers" of northeast New Delhi, who had taken to the streets in protest against the state's brutality. He tells the story of the night of December 15, 2019. An anti-CAA/NRC protest had taken place near Jamia Millia, and in an attempt to identify and arrest "vandals," New Delhi state police and paramilitary personnel had entered the university campus. They carried no warrant or paperwork detailing grounds for entry or arrest. It was a Sunday evening. Officers stalked into corridors after sunset, and, without warning, fired tear-gas shells and stun grenades. Students ran for cover, hiding behind upturned cabinets, shelves, desks. The police ransacked rooms, and broke tables and chairs. Dispatches from the scene overwhelmed social media: short, trembling videos evidenced the crushed glass and mangled metal covering the hallways, and the deafening, uninterrupted sound of tear gas shells. Walls were bloodstained. Later, witnesses spoke of hearing gunfire. In an act of cruelty designed to degrade its victims, state forces dragged praying students out of the university mosque, despite not being allowed to enter places of worship.

On stage in Amravati, Khalid explained how the stun grenades sounded like bombs, how the explosions reverberated for hours through the neighborhood, how the cloud of tear gas was so thick that even two kilometers from the campus, people's eyes watered when they stepped out of their homes, or opened windows. When residents tried to approach a local police station, they found that the doors were locked. "It was the grandmothers who found the courage," Khalid explains. A group of women led people to a sit-in site on the banks of the Yamuna River, in a neighborhood of New Delhi that would soon take over the Indian news feed—Shaheen Bagh. As Khalid speaks, the camera filming him—a mobile phone—clumsily pans across the crowd, showing the hundreds of men seated in the audience. Khalid addresses the congregation not as a lone revolutionary figure, staking an individual claim of leadership, but reiterates how Muslim women were leading the movement. It's nighttime, the crowd is seated on white plastic chairs and rugs laid on the ground. The area is enclosed by blue satin curtains. Audience members are clutching their phones, recording Khalid, periodically breaking into applause.

IV.

On March 2, 2020, politician Amit Malviya tweeted a forty-two-second-long extract from the video of Umar Khalid's Amravati speech. Malviya is a member of Modi's BJP, the Bharatiya Janata Party, which translates to the People's Party of India. "Umar Khalid, already facing sedition charges," Malviya writes alongside the video clip, "exhorted a largely Muslim audience to come out on the streets in huge numbers. ... Was the violence in Delhi planned weeks in advance?" In the extracted footage, Khalid simply says: since the state is trying to divide the country, people must come together to unite it. "Will you join me?" he asks the crowd. Republic TV, a right-wing media channel, prolific in amplifying fake news, picked up Malviya's edit of the video and broadcast it on primetime news, accusing Khalid of inciting a riot. In the charge sheet filed against Khalid, this video clip is listed as a reason for his arrest; it is a crucial piece of evidence. At a bail hearing in August 2021, Khalid's lawyer called Republic TV's decision to broadcast the truncated video the "death of journalism." When counsel asked the news channel where they sourced the footage from, they admitted it had been taken from Malviya's tweet. Far from being seditious, the full video of Khalid's speech is deeply moving footage, a testament to the dignity of those facing state subjugation. "The history of Jamia Millia, our history, is a history of sacrifices made for this country," Khalid says. "If you want to rain your sticks on us, if you want to shoot your guns, if you want to put us in jail, then go ahead, we are willing to make the sacrifice."

Not one police officer was prosecuted for the incident at Jamia Millia University. On December 21, 2019, journalists Shahid Tantray and Ahan Penkar interviewed Mohammed Minhajuddin, a young Jamia Millia student with a bruised and swollen eye for *The Caravan*, one of India's few independent political journals. In the video, Minhajuddin is sat at home in front of a blue patterned wallpaper, a prayer ringing through the air. A philosophy student, he explains to the camera how he ran into a library to take cover. The police broke windows to enter and hit him squarely in one eye with a wooden stick. His eye was instantly blinded. They were "fully prepared to attack students," he explains, "no talk, no interrogation, no questions were asked." After he was hit, Minhajuddin was taken into custody. When he asserted his legal right to record a statement, the police interrogated him instead of noting down what he said. According to reports, over 200 people were injured during the ambush, nearly all of them Muslim. Several nearby hospitals treated bullet wounds.

Two months after the Jamia Millia incident, in February 2020, the Jamia Coordination Committee, a student organization, released CCTV footage from that night. It shows armed paramilitary and police agents entering the Old Reading Hall dressed in camouflage combat gear, faces covered in scarves. They lean over desks and beat students working at computers or huddled over stacks of paper. Despite the narrative the state has maintained, the video proved, without a flicker of doubt, the sadism inflicted on students. "I'll end my message with this one appeal," says Khalid in the dispatch he recorded before his arrest. "Do not get scared."

V.

Umar Khalid and his comrades have been charged with the most severe offenses a nation-state can levy against its people, including terrorism, murder, and the manufacture and sale of arms. Nearly all of the activists have been charged with the Unlawful Activities (Prevention) Act (UAPA), which ambiguously determines what constitutes "terrorist activity." Given its interpretative definition, sections of the UAPA prove exceptionally difficult to petition against, especially for bail. On February 26, 2020, before the special cell of the Delhi Police began its flurry of activist arrests, four video clips were played in the Delhi High Court. The judges were conducting hearings to determine a response protocol. They confronted representatives of the Delhi Police, including the Deputy Commissioner, stating that the police had not taken sufficient action against violent perpetrators. The judges played the videos—all from the months leading up to the clashes—as evidence of the genesis of the attacks, marking the individuals in them as instigators. Each video was of a BJP party member rousing, or being involved in, the savagery that had taken over the city. The Delhi Police claimed to have never seen or heard of the videos, or what they depicted and, so, the judges put them on.

The first video, from late January 2020, was of Anurag Thakur, a BJP minister of state, addressing a large, agitated crowd. He is dressed in a saffron-colored scarf and stands in front of a poster of Home Minister Amit Shah, Modi's right-hand man. Shah's face is enormous, zoomed-in and blown-up. "Desh ke gaddaron ko," Thakur chants to the riled-up audience. *The traitors of this country.* The crowd responds: "Goli maron salon ko." *Let's shoot the bastards.* The second video was of an Asian News International (ANI) interview with BJP member of parliament Parvesh Sharma, also from late January. Sharma is seated at a desk, wearing a starched black waistcoat over a white shirt. The people of Shaheen Bagh, Sharma says, "will enter your homes, rape your sisters and daughters, kill them." His voice is clear, unwavering. He appears calm, speaks monotonously; he is entirely convinced of his accusations.

The third video was a clip of a demonstration held at the Maujpur metro station by BJP leader Kapil Mishra on February 23. Mishra stands flanked by a policeman in a bulletproof vest and wired helmet. He speaks to the crowd in no ambiguous terms; his speech is mutinous. He calls the protestors criminals and demands immediate punitive action. He directs attention to a sit-in led by a group of women at the next station on the metro, Jaffrabad, where the assembly was occupying a carriageway. He issues an ultimatum to the police: either clear out the Jaffrabad and nearby Chand Bagh protest sites, or his supporters would do it themselves. "We will be forced to descend into the streets," he declares. The crowd is provoked. Shortly after Mishra's speech, BJP supporters in the area—throngs of upper-caste Hindu men—started to throw stones, swing batons and iron rods. By early the next morning, there was an official estimate of eight people dead. The mobs were bloodthirsty; a group demolished the protest in Chand Bagh, as though taking a literal cue from Mishra's speech. They had used petrol bombs to set the site on fire. At midday, the police arbitrarily teargassed a women's sit-in tent in Kardampuri. The arson, stone-pelting, and shooting continued for the next four days, raging through the city's north-eastern neighborhoods. Both sides suffered casualties, as did the police. Mosques and car parks were burned down; journalists beaten up for attempting to do their jobs. A fourteen-year-old Muslim boy was hit by a stray bullet in the crossfire, wounded along his spine. It took six hours for an ambulance to reach him.

The last video played in court, taken on February 25, was a recorded excerpt of a Facebook Live broadcast by BJP official Abhay Verma, who live-streamed a scene from an alley at nighttime. Around him, a large group of enraged men—some wearing bright orange shirts, others covering their faces, lifting the cameras of their own mobile phones—chant violent obscenities. In the screen recording shown in court, blue "Like" and red "Heart" bubbles fill up the screen. After playing the videos, the court called for the arrest of Thakur, Sharma, Mishra, and Verma, and Justice S. Muralidhar critiqued the Delhi Police. Just a few hours after the judges had held three crucial hearings on the riots, Justice Muralidhar was transferred out of the Delhi High Court, the news announced close to midnight. By February 27, the Delhi Police began to arrest young activists instead, one of the first being Khalid Saifi, a charismatic orator. A few months on, it would be Umar Khalid's turn. In February 2021, Mishra—still roaming scot-free—will giddily declare to the press that, should he have to, "I will do what I did again."

VI.

Founding members of the feminist collective Pinjra Tod, Natasha Narwal and Devangana Kalita, were arrested by police on May 23, 2020, with charges similar to those that would be used to arrest Umar Khalid. Pinjra Tod, which translates as "break the cage," is comprised of students, both Muslim and Hindu. It was formed in 2015, at which time it had fifteen members and a Facebook page. Pinjra Tod describes itself as "an autonomous collective…fighting against the unjust and discriminatory regulations for women." Its members—many of whom see Narwal and Kalita as mentors, friends, sisters—are alumni and students at New Delhi colleges. Pinjra Tod began its life with a mission to oppose the patriarchy of the university system, and quickly evolved its position: the "patriarchy" in India cannot be separated from the politics of caste and religion. During the anti-CAA/NRC protests Narwal and Kalita addressed crowds and organized their networks to gather at protest sites, especially when numbers could strengthen attendees' resolve to face a police presence. Notably, the two had spoken at the Jaffrabad metro station sit-in, the one condemned by Kapil Mishra. They had communicated with each other, and members of Pinjra Tod, through WhatsApp. Their WhatsApp correspondence forms the New Delhi Police's primary case against them. In a statement, the police described them as "key conspirators" who "were guiding their foot soldiers" to commit "violence in the area."

Women pose a particular threat to the Modi regime and are specially targeted by its agents. Modi's government has steadily modeled itself on a trite masculinity. When he was first elected prime minister in 2014, he was presented as a benevolent patriarch. The 2014 election campaign slogan was "Acche din aane wale hain." *Good days are on their way.* Modi elicited a blind trust from an adoring public, who came to normalize each new diabolical policy or law and aggrandize their leader. News platforms would indulge in stories about the broadness of Modi's chest. In 2019, he filmed an epi-sode of *Man vs Wild* with stunt man Bear Grylls at the Jim Corbett National Park, a tiger reserve in the foothills of the Himalayas. The episode aired just days after the central government had sent 30,000 additional military troops into Jammu and Kashmir, revoking the state's special constitutional status, and installing a communications blackout. Women leaders, like those of Pinjra Tod—who remain poised and determined in their resistance against the Hindu patriarchy—upset and undermined the wretched masculinity that has otherwise been a mainstay of the Indian newsfeed.

During the anti-CAA/NRC protests, images of women gained a special currency. A few hours before the assault at Jamia Millia University on December 15, 2020, students had joined a protest march close to campus. When police infiltrated the picket line, protestors, fearing for their lives, fled into a nearby residential neighborhood. A group of students concealed themselves between two cars parked in front of the gate. A video, taken on an eye-witness' mobile phone, soon surged across social media: the police—once again dressed in bulletproof vests, helmets, and holding acrylic shields—pull a young man out onto the street. Five officers crowd over him, knock him to the ground, and beat him with their wooden sticks. Ladeeda Farzana and Ayesha Renna, friends of the victim, rush into the circle of policemen in an attempt to protect him. The police raise their batons to hit the girls as Renna moves to the center of the camera's frame. An officer strikes her leg but Renna, dressed in a deep red hijab, raises a single finger to him. "Move back," she says. This video went viral, and Renna's gesture lifted spirits; her pose of courage and resistance turned to one of hope. Her finger became a symbol of a large and complex movement.

Footage of women and young students from the protests—and their inevitable confrontations with state forces—moved from physical public space into the realm of the image, and thus into abstraction. Distant viewers—often "amplifying" certain stories on social media—used this abstraction to hold some kind of accountability, to reach some kind of resolve in the face of senseless and unending violence. Images turned into symbols, and symbols into representations of critical aspirations. These symbols hurtled through time and space, provoking nostalgia, rage, and even relief.

The Hindu right wing recognized the potential of such symbols. Shortly after the photographs and video of Farzana and Renna's intervention went viral, a smear campaign against Farzana was launched, and fake news circulated, attempting to incriminate her of spurring a riot. A doctored social media post was released, and a piece of fake pornography. *OpIndia*—a right-wing online news portal, which regularly circulates fake news—published a series of articles with accusations against Farzana. "Delhi violence started after Ladeeda's call to Jihad," reads one headline from August 2020. A month later, in September, Farzana filed a lawsuit against the website, condemning their reports as prima facie defamatory under the Indian Penal Code.

Modi's rebranded BJP has always had a strong command over media technologies. They ran an election campaign that used holograms to deliver speeches—their candidate materializing out of thin air like a divine spirit. These flickering appearances dazzled audiences, made Modi's presence ubiquitous. Crucial to the BJP's monopoly over the Indian media landscape are the operations of its "IT Cell," which produces propaganda in the form of fake news and colludes with social media platforms to disseminate it. Facebook, which owns WhatsApp, has been a key conspirator in this. As a *Wall Street Journal* article from August 14, 2020, reports, the company outright refused to regulate content posted by Modi's party and its officials. Ankhi Das, Facebook's Indian public policy executive, opposed hate-speech rules and "told staff members that punishing violations by politicians from Mr. Modi's party would damage the company's business prospects in the country." India is a "key market," and compliance with the party in power carries an economic imperative.

Prison is "the logical end of all the unfreedoms…one has been fighting against," Narwal wrote in a letter to members of Pinjra Tod from jail, "But I have seen—even in a place like this which is meant to strip away one's autonomy and humanity, reduce people to bare life—people still manage to retain some, hiding them in nooks and corners, hiding them from always prying eyes. They still manage to laugh, cry, sing together, form intimacies and friendships, dream about another future."

Khalid, Narwal, and Kalita are just three among the many others who have been framed under the Delhi riots case, or arrested in relation to their involvement with the anti-CAA/NRC protest movement. Parvez Ahmed, Shahdab Ahmed, Tasleem Ahmed, Akhil Gogoi, Meeran Haider, Tahir Hussain, Mohammed Ilyas, Sharjeel Imam, Ishrat Jahan, Athar Khan, Mohammed Saleem Khan, Saleem Malik, Khalid Saifi, Asif Iqbal Tanha, and Safoora Zargar are a few more. If local detentions and arrests are tallied across the country—of protest participants, outspoken people, writers, journalists, academics—the number goes upward of 3,000. "What is the risk I pose?" Khalid had asked in the video filmed before his arrest. The risk is perhaps this: daring to imagine, and attempting to realize, another future. "Sad yaad rakha jayega," says the opening line of an eponymous poem by young poet and actor Aamir Aziz. *Everything will be remembered*.

VII.

On December 20, 2020, Chandrashekhar Azad, leader of the Bhim Army, a Dalit resistance movement, issued a call to action. As part of the ongoing anti-CAA/NRC protests, he asked people to gather at the Jama Masjid in old New Delhi, a seventeenth-century Mughal mosque made from carved red brick. It was, at one point in history, the holiest site of Emperor Shahjahan's imperial seat. The police had been doggedly following Azad's movements, and even attempted to arrest him in advance of the protest. In old Delhi, a constable reached for the collar of his shirt. Azad escaped.

The police imposed Section 144 of the Criminal Procedure Code, which forbids the assembly of four or more people on the grounds of the potential for damage to human life or property, under the charge of rioting. It was a frantic move, and ultimately too late. Thousands had already begun to travel toward the mosque, from within New Delhi and from its two neighboring states, Haryana and Uttar Pradesh. By late afternoon, the steps of the mosque were overrun with people bent forward in prayer for the afternoon *namaz*. Media personnel and police officers had surrounded the gates of the mosque, standing outside, looking in, as though the scene were an elaborate performance. By law, police forces are not allowed to enter places of worship, so they circled the perimeter. The *azaan* rung across this impasse. It was met with the low rumble of water cannon engines. As the prayers ended, the crowd turned to face the cameras and the police, opening banners and flags, bursting into protest chants.

As cameras moved across the crowd, like owls hunting in the dark, Chandrashekhar Azad came into view, surrounded by a protective group of comrades, his lawyer behind him. He held up a copy of the Indian constitution: a document that protects the rights of citizens regardless of religion or caste. Every detail of this moment was enormously significant: Azad was surrounded by Muslim and Dalit protestors in solidarity with each other, gathered together in a historic Islamic city, on the steps of a mosque whose Persian name, Masjid-i-Jahan Numa, loosely translates to "a mosque that commands a view of the world." The copy of the constitution in Azad's hand had a photograph of the revolutionary leader Dr. B. R. Ambedkar on its cover. Dr. Ambedkar was a lawyer, economist, politician, and social justice reformer, and the writer of the Indian constitution. He had converted to Buddhism in a sharp critique and rejection of Hinduism and its embedded cruelty, particularly in how it devises, maintains, and rigorously upholds the caste system. Dr. Ambedkar wrote in legislature to override caste hierarchies and set affirmative action policies. The subcontinent, as structured by caste, had always been "essentially undemocratic," he said. He enabled a sophisticated set of reforms, those that were feminist, safeguarded the rights of laborers, and undermined caste monopoly over resources. In the present day, the Modi regime has instead emboldened casteist Hinduism, and all but granted impunity to its violent actors. As much as a contemporary Indian public, state, and judiciary deny the omnipresence of the caste system, India is still entirely governed by its tyranny.

The photograph of Dr. Ambedkar is crucial to understanding the significance of Azad's gesture. A return to the constitution was an obvious rebuttal to the state's rewriting of what the Constitution of India declares: that the Indian nation-state will not be governed by religious sentiments or majorities, and that the new republic's law will work toward the undoing of years of caste- and religion-based brutality. Yet Azad's gesture was not to return to a document that is otherwise enshrined within a narrative of decolonization, or of the first Indian prime minister Jawaharlal Nehru's vision for a "modern" India. It was instead an invitation to look at the constitution as an anti-caste document, and to see secularism not just as an ideological position, but as the only manner by which the Indian nation-state could begin to negotiate its overwhelming daily violence. The images taken of Azad, the protestors, and of Dalits and Muslims clutching the constitution, remind us that the end goal of resistance against the Modi regime is not to return to an India of the past, but to fundamentally reimagine the country we have inherited.

Watching the footage of that day was a visceral experience: history collapsed into the contemporary moment. Maulana Abul Kalam Azad, an Islamic theologist and India's first Minister of Education, had given an anti-Partition speech on the steps of the very same mosque in 1948. "I am an orphan in my own motherland," he had declared. While Partition sought to extract Muslim legacy from Indian soil, he had remarked on the impossibility of such a premise. "Remember," he said, addressing the Muslims present in the crowd, "Delhi has been nurtured with your blood."

VIII.

Since the 1990s, protests that take place in central New Delhi have often been corralled into the grounds of Jantar Mantar. The site is close to the parliament buildings, it's small enough to be managed by state forces, and with only two entrances and exits, it's easy to block off. Apart from its logistical value for the state, it makes for a surreal backdrop: Jantar Mantar—which translates to "calculating instruments"—is comprised of thirteen astronomy machines. Built in the early eighteenth century by a Rajput king, these large, stately red-brick structures are situated across the park, designed to predict the movements of the moon, the planets, and the sun. They are surreal objects with their many steps and curves, their ancient presence. Protesters gather amid this cosmological plain. Surrounding Jantar Mantar are several towering modernist buildings that remain from Nehru's time, in brutish stacks of concrete. The entire site—both cement and brick—is located in the heart of Lutyen's old colonial New Delhi and its neoclassical, grandstanding facades. Three visions of India are present in a single space, where they are met by an alternative: the public gathering of dissenting, critical, and impassioned Indian citizens.

The epicenter of the anti-CAA/NRC protest movement was the site in the neighborhood of Shaheen Bagh. Different from the grandstanding, formal architectures that are joined in Jantar Mantar, Shaheen Bagh is a Muslim locality comprised of mixed social classes. Up until the mid-1980s it was mostly farmland, but by the 1990s the land had been parceled off and sold for development projects. The first influx of new residents lived with open sewers, dirt roads, and poor electrical connections. Many were migrant laborers who had traveled to New Delhi from neighboring states. Over two decades, Shaheen Bagh became a dense, hybrid community of working- and middle-class inhabitants. In the days after the students of Jamia Millia University were attacked by state officials, four generations of locals spilled out into the streets in protest. A tent was put up to mark the center of the sit-in, mattresses and blankets laid out. People served "secular chai" and samosas.

In the discourse produced by the speeches, conversations, artworks, and poetry, the anti-CAA/NRC protests had begun to critically revisit the language that had, within the logic of the Indian nation-state, become sacred— words like "citizenship," "secularism," "democracy." Community leaders actively questioned this political jargon, which had largely been taken for granted, or left unexamined, by the mainstream since independent India was first formed. Citizenship and democracy, on some level designed to imply the safeguarding of populations, had turned monstrous. They also hinged on narratives of progress: since the formation of the Indian republic, in simply stating—and aestheticizing—conditions for progress, successive governments have maintained the illusion that progress is underway; that progress is the ultimate project of a postcolonial nation. The first aesthetic of this was conceived by Nehru's preoccupation with European modernism; the blankness of concrete was symbolic of change, aimed to imply an objective distance. It was the aesthetic bleaching of hundreds of years of casteist and Islamophobic history—concrete would symbolize the secular ideals of the new republic. Nehru had a great passion for cement, for dams, buildings, bridges; for a new, modern public infrastructure. Today, this concrete looks like poor camouflage. Both casteism and Islamaphobia remain visible in the architecture of most modern Indian cities: we occupy segregated landscapes, coded by layers of access and privilege. This makes the occupations of public space during the anti-CAA/NRC protests, and the protests that have come before them, all the more revolutionary.

After 2014, with the election of Modi's BJP, the narrative of progress was exponentially accelerated. "Acche din aane wale hain." *The good days are on their way.* They did not arrive. The social and economic structure of the nation lies in ruin, particularly with the constant addition of policies that seek to strip regional state governments of their autonomy and centralize all power. The handling of the COVID-19 crisis exemplified this: state governments were unable to enforce local lockdowns or specific healthcare policies, the central government filed petitions in the Supreme Court to make itself the sole proprietor of pandemic handlings. The Modi regime repeatedly lied in open court: about the deaths of migrant laborers who were rendered unemployed overnight after the declaration of the national lockdown; about the lethal shortage of oxygen during the deadly second wave. Despite an enormous death toll, and the total collapse of healthcare infrastructure, the regime actively ran a parallel operation to malign a non-violent people's movement. It has incarcerated the leaders of this movement under notorious and archaic laws, blindly characterizing young students as terrorists, as murderers, as manufacturers of arms. In doing so it not only criminalizes them—these spirited leaders—but has also taken away their capacity to do the work of holding space for public discourse and critique. The physical sites of the movement have been destroyed; its revolutionaries placed in prisons.

IX.

In August 2021, the Taliban took control of Afghanistan. As Afghans began to seek asylum, the Modi government seemed to issue "emergency visas" only to Hindus and Sikhs; the CAA was effectively put into action. Earlier the same month, at Jantar Mantar, a group of BJP supporters gathered in an anti-Muslim demo, children holding up posters calling for the "Annihilation of Islam." Thirty-four-year-old eyewitness Mohammad Nasir told *Al Jazeera* that Muslims in India live in "an atmosphere of perpetual fear." Nasir had lost an eye in the February 2020 clashes. On September 10, 2021, Nupur Thapliyal, a correspondent for *LiveLaw India*, tweeted an update from inside a courtroom hearing a petition in the Delhi riots case. "UAPA accused Khalid Saifi and his wife [are] exchanging smiles," writes Thapliyal. She describes how Saifi's daughter shows him how long her hair has grown since she last saw him, how she smiles.

In a July interview with Sharjeel Imam, one of the first activists and scholars to be arrested by the Delhi police in the riots case, *Article 14* asks, "What drove you to protest?" In response, Imam posits, "What drove millions of others to protest beside me?" It was only because of several petitions filed by Imam's lawyer—and nearly a year after the first request was made—that he was finally given access to the 17,000-page charge sheet levied by the Delhi Police against him. He expects to be held for up to seven years in pre-trial detention. Imam spends most of his time in solitary confinement in Tihar Jail, a maximum-security prison in New Delhi. He reads, he works on his PhD thesis, which is on Partition and the subcontinent's history of communal violence. One of the primary sources for his research, Imam explains in the interview, is his own charge sheet.

Natasha Narwal, Devangana Kalita, and Asif Iqbal Tanha were granted interim bail in the only glimmer of hope the riots case has seen so far. The New Delhi High Court wrote, "it is not uncommon for protestors to push the limits permissible in law," and, importantly, that this does not "amount to the commission of a 'terrorist act' or a 'conspiracy' or an 'act preparatory' to the commission of a terrorist act as understood under the UAPA." As Khalid had emphatically declared in his Amravati speech, "This fight is long." We must attend closely to the details. The fists, the upturned faces, the books, the drawings, the protest signs; the barricades, the tear-gas shells, the metal bullet casings, the batons, the speeding jets of liquid spouting from water cannons.

Images

Guwahati, India, December 11, 2019: Police fired teargas to demonstrators while protesting against the government's Citizenship Amendment Bill (CAB).

Guwahati, India, December 11, 2019: Police use water cannons to disperse demonstrators during a protest against the Citizenship Amendment Bill (CAB).

Shaheen Bagh area, New Delhi, India, January 23, 2020: An NGO by the name of India Reads, India Resists set up a study and painting area for the children whose mothers were taking part in the protests against the Citizenship Amendment Act (CAA) and National Register of Citizens (NRC).

Shaheen Bagh area, New Delhi, India, January 23, 2020: An NGO by the name of India Reads, India Resists set up a study and painting area for the children whose mothers were taking part in the protests against the Citizenship Amendment Act (CAA) and National Register of Citizens (NRC).

New Delhi, India, January 21, 2020: An art installation, "Map of India," with slogans against the controversial Citizenship Amendment Act (CAA), the National Register of Citizens (NRC), and the National Population Register (NPR) was erected in Shaheen Bagh.

Jamia Millia Islamia, New Delhi, India, December 15, 2020: Police attack students inside the university library.

Jamia Millia Islamia, New Delhi, India, December 15, 2020: Police attempt to smash the video cameras to prevent themselves from being filmed.

Mumbai, Maharashtra, India, April 14, 2014: People attend an election rally organized by the Bharatiya Janata Party, where, for the first time in the history of India, the party's prime ministerial candidate, Narendra Modi, addressed the audience via 3-D screens across 100 Locations in India simultaneously.

Mumbai, Maharashtra, April 14, 2014: An image of Narendra Modi pictured during a live "3-D hologram" broadcast. Modi, who addressed supporters earlier in a "talk over tea" election campaign, addressed Indians from Gandhinagar to some 100 locations across the country through this telecast.

New Delhi, India, December 15, 2019: Aysha Renna and demonstrators react against police violence during a protest against a new citizenship law.

Outside Jama Mosque, New Delhi, India, December 20, 2019: Bhim Army chief Chandrashekhar Azad, along with Indian Muslim activists during a protest against the Citizenship Amendment Act (CAA).

Acknowledgments

This essay, like every single one I have written, would not be what it is without the generous support and care of my friends whom I admire so greatly. Bikki, thank you for the gift of your sharp eyes. To Raj, for your honesty, and the small moments that gave me clarity. Adam, for teaching me so much about care. M, for running with me. To Adania and Lawrence, for a video call that sent me looking for a different future. Thank you En, for encouraging me to think differently, and to Tom, for sharpening my voice. Thank you, Izabella, I learn so much from the way your mind moves. Rosanna, it's difficult to put into words what you are, you are the very best of us. Thank you, Louisa for your thoughtfulness. Thank you to my publisher, Aaron, for the trust and patience, and for giving me the space to try this. To Arundhati, for the unwavering faith. Finally: I am in awe of, indebted to, and continuously inspired by, the journalism of *The Caravan*, *The Wire*, *LiveLaw.in*, *Scroll.in*, *The Kashmir Walla*, and every photographer and writer that continues to brave this moment in time, despite its claustrophobia and threat of violence. I take comfort, every day, that there is a community of us—even if we are yet to meet— who are joined together in the making of these records.

Biography

Skye Arundhati Thomas is a writer based in Goa, India. Her writing has appeared in *Artforum*, the *London Review of Books*, *Frieze*, and *ArtReview*, among other places. She is co-editor of *The White Review*.

Image Credits

P. 45
© David Talukdar / Imago images /
ZUMA Press

P. 46
© Anuwar Hazarika / REUTERS

P. 47
© Rajat Gupta / EPA-EFE

P. 48
© Rajat Gupta / EPA-EFE

P. 49
Photo by Mayank Makhija /
NurPhoto
© picture alliance / NurPhoto

PP. 50–51
© Maktoob Media

P. 52
© mauritius images / ZUMA
Press, Inc. / AlamyMaterial

P. 53
© Indranil Mukherjee / AFP via
Getty Images

P. 54
© Adnan Abidi / REUTERS

P. 55
© Rajat Gupta / EPA-EFE

Every effort has been made to
trace the copyright holders
and obtain permission to repro-
duce this material. The publisher apologizes for any errors
or omissions in the above list
and would be grateful if notified
of any corrections that should
be incorporated in future reprints
or editions of this book.

Colophon

Series editor:
Aaron Bogart

Editor:
Rosanna Mclaughlin

Editorial advisor and
copyediting:
Louisa Elderton

Proofreading:
Julie Astor

Graphic design:
Daniela Burger

Photo editor:
Josephine Kaatz

Reproductions:
Falk Messerschmidt

Typeface:
Kelvin Avec Clair

Printing:
druckhaus köthen

Paper:
Fedrigoni Constellation Snow,
Munken Print White

© 2021 Floating Opera Press,
Berlin, and the author

Published by
Floating Opera Press
Hasenheide 9
10967 Berlin
www.floatingoperapress.com

ISBN 978-3-9819108-6-5
Printed in Germany